The Wilds of Whip-poor-will Farm

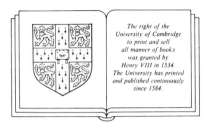

Published by the Press Syndicate of the University of Cambridge
The Pitt Building, Trumpington Street, Cambridge CB2 1RP
32 East 57th Street, New York, NY 10022, USA
10 Stamford Road, Oakleigh, Melbourne 3166, Australia

First published by Greey de Pencier Books, Canada 1982
©Janet Foster 1982
This edition first published by
Cambridge University Press, 1987

Printed in Canada

ISBN 0-521-35170-7 Hardcovers
ISBN 0-521-35968-6 paperback

The Wilds of Whip-poor-will Farm

True Animal Stories
by Janet Foster

Illustrated by Olena Kassian

Cambridge University Press
New York   New Rochelle   Melbourne   Sydney

Contents

MAY THEY ALWAYS BE WILD

All of the animals that live in these pages are real. They belong to their own wild world, and although many of them became very familiar to us during our first year at Whip-poor-will Farm, they were never tamed...they never became pets. And I am glad, for we love their wildness, and there is magic in quietly watching animals that live so separately from us, and in knowing that for a little while they have let us come into their world.

EAST FIELD

JUNIPER MEADOW

RIDGE TRAIL

DENSE
WOODS

UNKNOWN COUNTRY

BEAVER LODGE

DENSE WOODS

Howls in the Night

The sun shining on the side of the tent woke me up.
So did the delicious smell of the bacon and eggs
that John was frying up over the open fire. "C'mon,
lazy bones," he called out, "time to get going." It was a
warm, splendid September day. Dew glistened in the tall
grasses and the campfire smoke curled up into a clear
blue sky. Dressing quickly, I pulled on my work boots and
crawled out of the tent. What a marvellous day to start
building our new home!

Spread out all around our campsite in the open field were rows and rows of pine and cedar logs, each one carefully measured and marked. Our new home was going to be a small log cabin. We had cut the logs right on the farm, hauling the big trees out of the bush in the early spring and peeling them with an old tool called a drawknife which easily lifted off the stubborn bark. Then, lying in the field all summer, the logs had slowly dried and turned golden. Now it was autumn and we were all set to build.

We had chosen the cabin site carefully after inspecting every field, meadow and small clearing on the farm. Tucked into a long line of young maple trees at the edge of the East Field, we had found the perfect place. Here, the cabin would be facing south. There would be good views in all directions and we would be close enough to the woods to see all the wild creatures I hoped were living there. I couldn't wait to get started.

The logs were still very heavy and even the big

front-end loader of the tractor could barely lift them. Some of the pine logs weighed almost half as much as the tractor itself. One by one, we set each log in place, shaping and fitting the corners together and chinking the small cracks between the logs with a soft insulating material to stop the wind from whistling through. Slowly, log by log, the walls went up and our cabin began to take shape.

It was hard work, building our own home, but it was great fun too. Each night we sat around the campfire drawing diagrams and trying to decide how big the windows should be, where the doors would go, how much insulation we needed for the ceiling and where the woodstove would sit. There was so much to think about and so much to plan.

We worked long hours every day and by the end of the first week we were exhausted. On Friday night, I could hardly keep my eyes open long enough to finish supper. The tent had never looked so inviting. Curled up warm and snug in my sleeping bag, I was just falling asleep, my mind already half dreaming, when I heard a thin, high-pitched howl. It was a strange, eerie wail. As the call faded away, a second one rose in answer, beginning with an ear-piercing "yip, yip, yip," then a long, moaning howl. These weren't the voices of neighbouring dogs! I rolled over in my bag and nudged John. "Listen!" But he was already wide awake. "Coyotes," he whispered. "They're in the East Field." Now the wild voices came together in a duet of yips, barks and howls that lasted a full minute. Then, silence.

We had known there were coyotes on the farm when we bought it, for we had seen their large tracks in the soft ploughed earth at the edge of the fields. And once, in

the early evening, I had caught just a glimpse of a
shadowy grey form melting into the woods as I crossed
the wide Centre Field. But we had never heard them howl
before. I wondered if they were proclaiming their territory
or calling out to find each other. Or maybe they were
just feeling good! Our neighbours call the coyotes brush
wolves, for they are first cousins to the larger timber
wolves of the North. But I've always loved the name the
Indians first gave them: God's dogs.

I lay awake in the tent and listened for a long time,
hoping the coyotes would sing again. But the concert
was over.

Next morning, I scrambled out of the tent and ran
across the field in the direction the howls had come

from. Sure enough, on a
bare patch of ground I found fresh
tracks. They showed up clearly on the damp
earth, and from the number of paw prints I knew there
had been two coyotes, maybe even three. Their tracks
were neater and slightly smaller than those of a big dog,
and they ran almost in a straight line beside the cedar
rail fence down to the corner of the field. The coyotes
must have been hunting. In our area of southern Ontario
they live mostly on small animals, such as rabbits and
mice, and even birds if they can catch them. I followed
the tracks, but lost sight of them when they passed under
the fence and turned into the woods. The coyotes had
passed by so close to us! I felt a shiver of excitement.

Would they come again? Did they know we were camped in the field? Did they only howl at night? Were they afraid of us? The questions tumbled around and around in my head, but I set my mind to thinking. There must be a way we could meet these wild and mysterious visitors....

We knew that coyotes were not the only wild creatures that lived on our farm. A groundhog surveyed us solemnly from the top of a large rock beside his burrow in the West Field as we banged and hammered away on the cabin. Perhaps he was wondering who his new neighbours were. When he wasn't sunning himself or watching us, he was down feeding on the rich red clover and alfalfa that grew in the field. We called him Rufus and all during September he became fatter and fatter. Sometimes I would stop work and glance over just in time to see Rufus diving into his burrow. A few moments later he would pop up again from another entrance part way up the hill. With his network of underground tunnels and different burrows, we never knew when, or where, Rufus was going to appear next!

18   There were also porcupines on the farm, and at least two of them loved the red clover as much as Rufus did. Late each afternoon they appeared like two dark lumps in the field, shuffling up through the tall grass to their favourite clover patch near the cabin. They ate noisily, smacking their lips together and swallowing the juicy plants flowers and all. Porcupines don't dig burrows and hibernate the way groundhogs do, and I wondered where these two were going to spend the winter.

We soon discovered that the porcupines liked more than just clover. A loud chewing noise awakened us one night. The sound was so loud it seemed to be coming from right outside the tent. I shone my flashlight out and there was Porky, happily chewing away on one of the expensive plywood sheets we had bought for the cabin roof. "Hey!" I yelled. Startled, Porky dropped the plywood and waddled off around the side of the cabin into the darkness, chattering his teeth together and protesting loudly. "We'd better nail that roof up first thing in the morning," I muttered to John as I crawled back into my sleeping bag. I remember thinking just as I dropped off to sleep, what would Porky do to our logs? I had a feeling we were going to find out!

By the end of September, our cabin was nearly finished. Just in time, too, for it was getting cold in the tent at night. Early one morning, I poked my head out the door and found our campsite buried beneath a blanket of wet snow! The snow melted away quickly once the sun rose above the trees, but it was a sign that winter was on the way. Rufus had already disappeared down his burrow to begin a long winter sleep, and we had heard the first flocks of wild geese heading south. One flock passed so

low over our camp that I could hear the thump, thump of their wings beating the air.

On the very last day of September, we finished the cabin. We worked long and hard all that day, cleaning and sweeping out the inside, checking between the logs for tiny cracks that needed to be sealed, sanding and painting the window frames bright red, and fitting pine planks together to make the doors. We worked so hard we forgot all about lunch. But by the end of the day, everything was ready. Down came the tent and we moved into our house of trees.

What a wonderful feeling, to be living in a house we had built ourselves. I could look around and recognize each log in the walls, remembering where it had been felled, how easily it had peeled, and how difficult it had been to put up. The cabin glowed inside from the rich colour of the logs and we felt a wonderful sense of achievement. It had been well worth the hard work and tired muscles.

That night, we lit the woodstove and had supper by candlelight on a small table under the window. Outside, the night was clear and very cold. Not a breath of wind stirred the branches of the maple wood. As the full moon rose over the trees, it cast long shadows across the field. I opened the cabin door and slipped quietly out. Everything was peaceful and still. A dog barked once, far away, and I remembered the coyotes. Where were they now? Somewhere deep in the woods or just over there in the shadows at the edge of the field? And then it came to me: maybe I could find out where the coyotes were by calling to them! Once when we were camping in the North, John had howled and been answered by timber wolves. My voice was not nearly as deep as John's, but then neither was a coyote's. If I could just give the right call, they might think I was another coyote and respond. It was certainly worth a try.

I took a deep breath and gave out a long, lingering howl, hitting a high note and then letting my voice slide down all the way to a whisper: "Ahooowwwwwwwwwwwwwwww...."

I waited, straining my ears in the silence, but no one answered. "Try again," John murmured behind me. "Maybe they're farther away." This time I gave three barking yips before the long, drawn-out howl, but still

there was no response. I felt disappointed. We would
have to find some other way of making contact with
these wild creatures. "Come on," John encouraged, as I
began to turn away, "One last time."

Closing my eyes tight, I put everything I had into my
howl, trying to strike the same mysterious and haunting
chord the coyotes had done the night we listened to
them from the tent. And even before I had finished, the
answer came back in a great crescendo of howls, yips
and barks that tore the silence apart. The entire family
was responding from the Centre Field just beyond the
wood. We recognized the voices of the parents and the
thin, high-pitched yipping of the pups. As each howl
ended, another began, until the whole night was filled
with coyote song. On and on the wild chorus went. When
the singing stopped, I howled once more and the family
started up all over again, barking and howling in answer.
I was fairly dancing up and down with excitement.

Then, as suddenly as they had begun, the voices fell
silent. I howled and howled but there was no answer.
Once again, the nightly concert was over. But this time
we had been a part of it! God's dogs had given us a
proper welcoming to Whip-poor-will Farm.

Whiskers and Friends

Now that we were living in the cabin, we spread thick rugs, built kitchen counters and stored enough firewood in the woodshed to last us through the coming winter. Our new log home was soon warm and cozy, but I did notice that it was not very

quiet at night. Every evening, just after dark, we began to hear loud creaking noises and strange little scratching sounds, particularly in the area of the kitchen. At first we thought it was merely the sound the logs made as they settled in the walls. Some of the big pine logs had not dried enough during the summer and the sap inside them was still wet. As the logs continued to dry in the cabin, they shrank and settled, opening up small cracks between the logs that had to be filled. The sound of the logs settling would certainly account for the odd creaking noises we heard, but not the mysterious little scratching sounds. There had to be another explanation.

One night I was curled up reading in the big armchair
in front of the fire. Just as I turned the page, my eye
caught a sudden movement at the far end of the room.
Something was moving the kitchen curtains. I looked up,
startled. The window wasn't open and the curtains were
hanging straight and still. Were my eyes playing tricks on
me? Deciding the wind must have blown through a crack
in the wall that I had not filled, I went back to my book.

Then it happened again. Getting up, I tiptoed across
the cabin into the kitchen and yanked the curtains open.
Clinging to the narrow ledge of the window pane was a
small, grey deermouse with large, round ears, bright
black eyes and very long whiskers. Surprised, we stared
at each other, but before I could say a word, the mouse
ran lightly down the logs, scampered across the floor and
disappeared behind the bookcase. He seemed to know
exactly where he was going. Now I knew who had made

the little scratching sounds, but how had the mouse got into the cabin?

Taking a large brown paper bag, I scattered a handful of peanuts inside and laid the bag on the floor. Deermice have a remarkable sense of smell, and it didn't take long for Whiskers to come out from behind the bookcase, his nose twitching. Cautiously, he began to cross the rug toward me, his eyes fixed firmly on the paper bag. When he was so close that I could see the silken hairs on his tiny paws, he stopped and looked up at me inquisitively. Then he stared right into the big bag and all of his long whiskers began to quiver. He wanted those peanuts! I waited until the tip of his tail had disappeared inside, then I grabbed the bag with both hands, holding the top tightly closed. Carrying my little captive triumphantly outside, I released him into the hedgerow and he scooted away among the rocks.

Feeling rather pleased with myself, I went back into the cabin, put another log on the fire, picked up my book and settled down to read once more. But I had not finished a single page before the kitchen curtains were moving again. Whiskers had come back! I soon found his entrance, a narrow crack between two logs above the kitchen window. It was an opening just large enough for a very small mouse to squeeze through. And then we discovered Whiskers wasn't the only mouse moving in. An entire family of deermice had decided our warm, cozy cabin was just the place to spend a long, cold winter!

We successfully sealed up every crack and opening we could find in the logs, but the mice had other trails leading up into the roof and down into the basement from the outside, trails so secret and so well hidden that we never did find them all. Whiskers and his friends were here to stay.

The basement was a perfect home for the mice and 27
at night they explored every corner of it. They ran along
the overhead wires, slid down the skis in the corner,
squeezed in and out of the drawers and tried to steal the
birdseed that was stored in metal containers. It took
them no time at all to learn the contents of every box
and jar on the crowded shelves. They hid sunflower seeds
in the toes of our boots and built their winter nests in
the soft insulation of the basement ceiling.

We were never quite sure just how many mice had
moved in for the winter. Sometimes it seemed that our
basement was overrun. One night I sat on the stairs and
counted at least nine mice. There were three, however,
that we came to know well–Misca, who was small and
mischievous, Tuffy, who was bold and had a short tail,
and Whiskers, who turned out to be a Mrs. Whiskers in
the spring! All of the basement mice were charming,
sociable little creatures and we really did not mind
sharing our cabin with them. We lived upstairs and the
mice lived downstairs, where they were safe from hawks
and owls–and coyotes.

Then someone else moved in. We were sitting up in
bed sipping hot mugs of tea early one morning when we
heard a loud *clunk.* I thought the noise came from the
woodshed, but John insisted it had come from the
basement. We tossed the question back and forth, neither
of us willing to get out of the warm bed long enough to
solve the mystery, and then the noise came again. "Why
don't you go down and see what it is" John suggested
brightly, pointing out that my side of the bed was closer
to the basement than his. Grumbling, I reluctantly shoved
aside the blankets, padded across the cold floor in my
bare feet and raised the trap door to the basement. The
noise was probably nothing more than Tuffy knocking

something over, I thought as I went down the stairs. But the moment I switched on the light, I saw a furry animal running like a white streak back and forth on the wooden beam above the basement window. His face was small, his winter coat was the colour of polished snow and there was a black tip at the end of his tail. It was an ermine! My excited cry brought John pounding down the stairs behind me.

The ermine was agile and moving very fast. One minute he was high on the top shelf looking down at us inquisitively, the next moment he was gliding across the floor. His slender body was much longer than that of a mouse, but he could slip just as quickly and easily through the smallest openings. My eyes could hardly keep up with the speed of his travels.

We had no idea how long the ermine had been in the basement, or how he had found his way in. Ermine are members of the weasel family and they live on deermice and other small rodents. It was quite possible that this one had been hunting our mice outside and had chased them along their secret trails right into the basement. And where were the mice?

We had to catch the ermine as fast as we could. I was desperately afraid Tuffy and Whiskers would suddenly appear and that would be the end of them! We had bought a live trap, a little cage designed to catch small animals without hurting them, and quickly I set and baited it with juicy bacon. The ermine must have been very hungry, for as soon as we placed the trap on the floor, he excitedly ran all over it, smelling the bacon and madly trying to find his way inside. Finally, the ermine found the entrance, ran through, and the door closed automatically behind him.

Now most animals are very frightened when they are
caught in a live trap, but not the ermine—or "Herman,"
as John named him. He was far too busy gobbling up the
bacon to worry about his loss of freedom. I was delighted
to see how hungry he was because it meant he had not
eaten our mice! But once Herman had finished the bacon,
there was no mistaking that he wanted to get out. He ran
round and round in the confined space, fastening his
sharp teeth on the wire and trying to chew his way
through. It was time to let him go.

We released Herman near the woodshed, and he
streaked away between the rows of firewood. He had not
been harmed by his experience with us, but I had no
doubt that it would be a long time before we saw him
near the basement again!

That night the basement was very quiet. I watched
and waited, but there was no sign of the mice. Surely
they must have known the ermine was in the basement
and managed to escape outside in time. But why didn't
they come back, now the danger was passed? I sat at the
top of the stairs until long after bedtime. Just when I was
giving up all hope, a little grey mouse with very long
whiskers came running across the floor. He carried a
huge peanut in his mouth, and when he looked up at me
I was sure there was a twinkle in his black, shiny eyes.
There must have been one or two trails so secret and
safe that not even Herman could find them. Happily, I
closed the trap door and went to bed.

Porky's Home

The old barn had sat on top of the hill overlooking the field for well over a hundred years. There were holes in the roof and no glass in the windows. The doors had fallen off their hinges years ago and, on one side, the barn's stone foundation wall was slowly crumbling away. Rain seeped in through every crack and when the north wind blew, the floorboards creaked so loudly I thought someone was walking across the upstairs loft. We needed a home for our tractor but the barn seemed too old and too rundown for us to even try to repair it. I was afraid the next big storm would blow it over.

"Why don't we take it down," I suggested to John one autumn day, thinking we could build something useful from the lumber, maybe a small shed for the garden tools. John agreed. We might even be able to salvage some of the barn rafters if they were not too far gone. Putting on hard hats, we armed ourselves with wrecking bars and set out to begin the big job.

While John began prying up the floorboards inside, I walked around the barn on the outside until I found a small space where two big limestone blocks had fallen out of the wall. Lying flat on the ground, I wriggled between the blocks, squeezed through the narrow opening and dropped down into the dark basement. Cobwebs brushed past my face and water dripped from the low ceiling into icy puddles on the earthen floor. Everything smelled dank and musty.

As I crept forward, a low chattering sound came from the far end of the basement. I peered into the gloom and could just make out a large, dark lump. There was something very familiar about the shape of the lump. Perched on top of a pile of rubble in the far corner was a porcupine. He blinked his small eyes in the sudden glare

from my flashlight and clicked his teeth together in a loud warning. So this was where Porky had chosen to spend the winter – in the basement of our old barn!

Porky seemed none too pleased by my arrival. Maybe he was remembering the night I yelled at him from the tent when he was eating our plywood. Slowly and awkwardly he backed down off the rubble pile and began shuffling toward the opposite corner, chattering all the way. As I drew closer, his chattering became louder still, and the long quills that lay hidden among the soft hairs on his back and head rose up until he looked like a very annoyed pincushion. From the way he squinted at me through the gloom, I could tell Porky's eyesight was not very good. But there was nothing wrong with his hearing.

34 I had only to make the slightest sound with my foot and his quills rose even higher.

I tried to get a good look at the porcupine's face, close up, but each time I moved around into position, he turned and presented me with a good view of his back and all those quills! And when I stepped closer, he lashed his powerful tail from side to side like a big club. It too was covered with long quills, and at this moment they were all very much erect! I moved hastily back and kept my distance. One swipe of that tail and my boot would be full of quills.

Porky had been living in the old barn for quite some time. Maybe he spent every winter there. His small, pigeon-toed tracks had made well used trails across the dirt floor and up through the same narrow opening in the wall that I had crawled through. No doubt he slept down here during the day and went out at night to search for food.

Leaving Porky safely inside his winter den, I crawled back the way I came and announced to John that the barn was occupied. "I know," he said, "I've just found the skunk's entrance. He's living under the floor on the far side." "A skunk!" I yelled, "I meant the porcupine!" Then we discovered that Porky and the skunk were not the only residents. Climbing up the rickety stairs into the loft, I came face to face with a racoon, curled up on the warm straw. He too was moving in for the winter. Then I noticed the old swallow and phoebe nests clinging to the rafters. The birds used the barn in the spring and summer. And then John pulled away part of the wall and found a whole family of deermice living inside....

That settled it. The old barn was certainly not coming down. It was a home for too many wild creatures. In fact,

after much prodding and prying about, we realized it would be far simpler to fix it up than to tear it down. Besides, the floor at one end was still quite sound, so the barn would be a good home for our tractor after all. We needed no further justification.

The barn's future was secure. Instead of using our tools to tear it down, we built it back up. We put on a steel roof, hung new doors, replaced all the rotten beams, boarded over the holes, strengthened the floor and covered all the windows with clear plastic to keep out the icy winds.

Porky did not enjoy the rebuilding at all. I could hear his loud grunting as I hammered away upstairs. And while John struggled with the heavy cedar posts to bolster the basement ceiling, Porky sat in his corner, chattering his teeth and scolding continually. He must have thought his home had been invaded.

By the time the first heavy snows of winter arrived, the barn was in pretty good shape. With luck, it might last for another hundred years. Our tractor fitted in perfectly and would keep nice and dry all winter. The basement wall was repaired, but I made sure that we left a small entranceway so that Porky could come and go freely. Each night he ventured out, travelling down past the apple tree, through the fence (where he always left a few tell-tale quills sticking in the cedar rails), across the snowy field and into the wood. He followed the same route night after night all through the winter until his winding trails looked like tiny, well-ploughed highways.

I often wondered if Porky liked what we had done to the old barn. Certainly we had given him a secure home and one that was in no danger of falling down. I hoped that he appreciated our efforts. I also hoped that he did not mind sharing the barn with our big tractor. "Don't worry," John said. "Porky lives downstairs. He probably doesn't even know it's there." But later that winter we were in for a surprise. "What are all those funny looking marks on the tractor tires?" I asked, pointing to strange scrapes and gouges all over the heavy rubber. "Oh, no," John moaned, "Porky's been chewing the tires." I began to laugh. It was just Porky's way of reminding us that the old barn was his home first.

The Secret Lake

W e always knew there was a lake hidden somewhere in the woods far to the south of our cabin, but we had never seen it. It was so small that it had never been given a proper name and its tiny heart shape appeared on only a few of the larger county maps. Maybe that's why the local people seldom showed much interest in it. "Too small for fishing," some of them said. Our neighbour told us he'd seen the lake once, but that was a long time ago, and he couldn't even remember how he had come across it while he was logging in the dense bush. "Country changes a lot," he admitted, stroking his chin thoughtfully. "Don't reckon it would be easy to find now." I wasn't discouraged. I knew that somewhere, lost in the deep, dark woods at the very back of our land, there was a secret lake waiting to be found.

On a cold, clear day in late autumn, just as the maple leaves were beginning to turn crimson and frost tickled our fingers and noses, we bundled up and set off with a compass to find the little lake.

The first part was easy. Passing through the old gate below the cabin, we picked up Rabbit Trail, which wound through the tall stands of cedar and skirted the woods at the edge of the Centre Field. It had been an old cattle trail once and now we called it Rabbit Trail because the snowshoe rabbits liked to use it too.

Once past the Centre Field, we followed the Birch and Maple Wood trails through the forest and then we turned and hiked up along the High Ridge Trail. A red squirrel scolded us from the top of a tall spruce tree and little bands of black-capped chickadees flitted among the branches searching for tiny seeds. I brushed past a low juniper bush and startled a ruffed grouse that was roosting underneath. As the frightened bird rose into the

air, its wingbeats
made such an
explosion of noise
that for a second or two
my heart stopped.

After we left High Ridge
the woods became much deeper and
darker. The trails had ended. Now we were on our own,
and it was time to consult the compass. We struck out in
a southeasterly direction, having taken a rough bearing
while back at the cabin of where we thought the lake
should be. As long as we continued in more or less a
straight line, we would come to the secret lake, or so we
hoped. But it was tough going. Our route led through
thickets of prickly ash bushes that scratched our cheeks
and tore at our clothing, past cedar swamps so thick we
could hardly find our way through. We scrambled over
giant rocks and boulders left by an ancient glacier and
hopped across fast-flowing streams. We hiked through
pine groves that were as still and silent as cathedrals,
past maple trees so big I couldn't reach my arms around

their trunks. And we saw birch trees so white and
gleaming they must have been freshly scrubbed that very
morning.

On and on we went, always checking our direction
against the compass and wondering if we were ever going
to reach the secret lake.

Then, from a small clearing on top of a low hill
where we paused to catch our breath, I saw something
sparkling through the trees ahead. We were there!

Racing each other through the last dense cedar
swamp, we pushed aside the heavy branches and burst
out onto the grassy banks of the little lake. It was as
smooth as glass and ringed with golden tamarack trees.
The water was clear and very deep. A small school of
sunfish lazily swam by close to shore, their brightly
coloured scales flashing in the sunlight. They stayed and
watched us for a moment or two and then, with a flick of
their tails and feathery fins, cruised slowly on. A painted
turtle struggled up through the thick carpet of underwater
vegetation and hung motionless on the surface until my
sudden movement sent it diving for the bottom again.
One or two late season dragonflies skimmed low over the
water, and on shore, a huge green bullfrog solemnly

surveyed the lake with glassy, gold-rimmed eyes.

The lake was very quiet. Only the sound of a woodpecker drumming on a dead tree somewhere back in the woods broke the silence. Fumbling in my pack for the binoculars, I scanned the far side of the lake. Something close to shore was rippling the reflections. I carefully focused the binoculars on a small, dark head that was moving through the still water, leaving a familiar "v" of spreading ripples. Trailing behind was a long,

freshly cut, leafy poplar branch. A beaver was busy laying in his winter store!

As we watched, the beaver swam to the centre of the lake and then veered across toward a narrow point of land on our left. Just as it reached the shore, there was a loud splash and both beaver and branch disappeared under the water. I examined the point carefully with the binoculars and saw a huge mound of sticks at the edge of the shore. "It's the beaver's house," I whispered to John, handing him the binoculars.

Quietly we began to make our way around the bay. The shoreline was well flooded and there were deep channels cut in the bank where poplar branches had been dragged into the lake. Not far from the lodge we looked down into the clear water and saw the beaver's food supply, a great pile of twigs and branches poked carefully into the side of the bank. In winter, when the lake froze over, the beaver would be able to swim underwater from the lodge to the food store without having to come up through the ice.

As we reached the beaver lodge, there was a sudden rippling of the water and a beaver appeared. This was not the same one I had seen through the binoculars. It was much smaller and I decided it had to be the female. She floated on the surface just a short distance from us, then, leaving scarcely a ripple, dived. A few moments later, she surfaced near the middle of the lake and swam off toward the far shore. Climbing out onto the bank, she shook the beads of water from her matted fur and waddled off into the bushes. I had an idea she was going for more poplar branches. We were lucky to see the beaver at all for normally they work only at night. But perhaps they were working overtime to get their winter food supply in before freeze-up.

The beaver lodge was a giant mound of sticks and branches all woven together and held with mud. It sat at the edge of the lake and the beavers' hidden entrance was a long channel that led in from the lake and disappeared between two tree roots under the bank. The tunnel would lead right up into the middle of the house so that the beaver could come and go from the lodge without ever being seen.

I wanted to take an even closer look—the male beaver was still inside—but John quickly motioned me away and pointed out into the lake. The female was coming back. There was no place to hide so we just crouched down on the bank and waited.

She swam steadily toward us, holding her nose well above water and trailing a leafy poplar branch even longer than the one her mate had brought back. Suddenly she stopped swimming. Letting go of the branch, she turned her wet head from side to side, sniffing the air. I tried to sink even lower into the grass, but it was no good. A sudden breeze had come up and it was carrying our scent straight toward her. The beaver dived, and this time, as she rolled forward, the top of her flat broad tail hit the water with a resounding *whack!* that echoed clear across the lake. It was the beaver's warning signal to her mate.

We waited a long time, but the beaver did not surface again. "C'mon," John finally said as the sun sank lower and lower in the sky. "She's probably back inside the house by now. We'd better find our way back before dark."

And that's how the secret lake officially came to be known as Beaver House Lake! We went back again and again, finding easier routes every time and tying strands of brightly coloured wool on the trees to mark the trail.

44   Just before Christmas, we snowshoed in and crossed over the frozen lake to the lodge, now buried beneath a mound of fresh snow. A long line of fox tracks circled the lake and ran right over the top of the beaver house. But there was no reason to fear for the beaver. They were safely down inside the lodge and their underwater food supply was within easy swimming distance. We would not see them again until the ice melted in spring.

An Unexpected House Guest

Whoosh—something sailed down over the roof of the cabin, brushed past my ear with a soft rush of air and landed silently among the trees of the hedgerow. In the light from the cabin window I saw a small, pale shape with a flat, furry tail run up the trunk of a young maple. When it reached the fork in the tree, it paused and looked down at me with huge round black eyes, eyes that could see in the dark. It was a flying squirrel, and I knew what he wanted. I had just finished filling the big bird feeder in front of the cabin with fresh millet, cracked corn, peanuts and sunflower seeds.

Climbing even farther up the tall tree, the squirrel crawled out right to the end of a high branch, gathered himself into a tight ball and leapt out into space. Spreading all four feet and using his flat tail like a rudder, he glided smoothly and effortlessly toward the bird feeder. I could see the thin fold of skin stretching from his wrists to his ankles that allowed the squirrel to "fly" so easily through the air. He looked like a furry handkerchief with a tiny paw at each corner. Down he sailed, landing with a gentle plop on the snowy roof, and quickly disappeared inside the bird feeder.

I didn't have to look at my watch to know that it must be 8:30. The flying squirrel arrived for his supper each night at the same time. And he never ate alone. A few minutes later, his mate came gliding down too. They sat side by side, shelling the peanuts and husking the sunflower seeds with delicate, quick-moving fingers. Their brown, silky coats gleamed in the light from the cabin.

Sometimes when the squirrels arrived or left very suddenly, they startled the mice who were on the tray at the cabin window. Perhaps, when the squirrels glided through the air, the mice thought they were owls. It was very dangerous for the mice outside at night, and they knew it. But, like the squirrels, they had to store food for the winter. Besides, they could not resist the delicious smell of the peanuts. Tuffy's favourites were sunflower seeds. Stuffing his cheeks until they bulged, he would jump off the tray and race around the corner of the cabin, his paws leaving tiny footprints in the snow. I knew the little thief was heading for the basement and that somewhere in behind the shelves he was hoarding a great pile of husked sunflower seed.

The cabin window was my window on the wild world. Every night I watched all the comings and goings outside. One time I saw a saw-whet owl perched in the birch tree. I was worried about the flying squirrels, but the owl was hunting for mice. Luckily for the mice, he never seemed to have much success, at least not while I was watching.

There was even more activity around the cabin during

the day. Blue jays were usually the first to arrive for breakfast, and their loud, raucous calls soon brought everyone else. Chickadees, redpolls, tree sparrows, nuthatches and nearly a hundred golden evening grosbeaks flocked to the feeding stations. Red squirrels came too, scolding one another, and everyone else, so loudly while they ate that I often wondered why they never suffered from indigestion. Maybe they did.

On very cold mornings, the chickadees arrived with all their feathers fluffed up to keep them warm. They looked like round balls of cotton wool with just two black eyes and a beak peeking out. It was their way of putting on extra parkas, and we could always tell how cold it was outside by how big the birds looked!

In the middle of January, during the very coldest part of winter, we closed up the cabin and went away for two weeks. I hated leaving. The flying squirrels and the birds had come to depend on our food. What would happen if the supply ran out? I filled the big feeder right to the very top, hung great chunks of fatty suet from the tree branches and covered the window tray with so many seeds and peanuts that the birds would be standing knee deep. I hoped there would be enough for everyone. We let the fire die out in the cabin, drained the water pipes, shuttered all the windows and locked the doors.

The whole time we were away, it snowed and snowed and snowed, and the temperature fell lower and lower. By the time we arrived back, huge snowdrifts were piled around the cabin and the lane had completely disappeared. As we snowshoed in from the road, I scanned the trees anxiously, but there were no birds in sight. Maybe it was too late in the day. We unlocked the back door and went inside. It was freezing cold and pitch dark.

I was just taking off the shutter from the west window when John called out behind me, "Don't move. There's a squirrel on the floor!" Easing the heavy shutter down, I slowly turned and saw the flying squirrel on the carpet just behind me. It was a miracle I had not stepped on him when I came in. His big, luminous eyes were barely open and his once glossy fur was dull and drab. I knelt and reached out but, weak as the small creature was, he skittered away into the corner on wobbly legs. There he sat, hunched over and scarcely moving.

I looked around the cabin, wondering how the squirrel had managed to get in, then noticed the door of the fireplace was open just a crack. The squirrel must have fallen down the chimney. Thank heavens the fireplace door was not locked. But how long had he been inside the cabin?

Quickly, John sprinkled some nuts and seeds into a small saucer and held it out. For the longest time there was no movement from the furry bundle, but then two little paws reached out and closed firmly around a peanut. I breathed a sigh of relief.

The flying squirrel was half-starved. All that had kept him alive were a few seeds that had fallen on the kitchen

52 floor. But because he had no water, he would not have lived for very much longer. We filled a small egg cup and the squirrel drank and drank until there was not a drop left. He was so weak and so thirsty that he must have been locked inside the cabin for at least three days, maybe longer. If we had come back just one day later it might have been too late.... I tried not to think about it.

Our next job was to make our visitor a nest for the night, one that would be as warm as his own. Finding a small wooden box, John cut a hole in one end for an entrance and I filled the box with soft paper and placed it in a large glass aquarium. Then, I gently picked up the flying squirrel. He did not resist and felt so soft in my hand that it was like holding a small ball of wool. A warm nest was just what he wanted, for the moment I set him down he disappeared into a cloud of Kleenex inside the box.

That night the cabin was still quite cool so we kept the aquarium close to the fire. Once or twice I shone my flashlight over, but the squirrel was sound asleep inside his box. I knew he had eaten well, for the peanuts and sunflower seeds we had left in the aquarium were all gone.

Next morning the wind was up and it was bitterly cold. The flying squirrel was still weak, but his eyes were almost wide open now and he was more alert. The sooner we could get him back to his own nest, the better he would be. His mate must have been wondering where he had gone.

Right after breakfast we put on scarves and parkas and snowshoed down to the woods, carrying the flying squirrel in his box. Having no idea where the nest was, we could only hope that the woods would be familiar and that the squirrel would be strong enough to find his own way home. Choosing a big maple tree, John tipped the box against the trunk and out tumbled the squirrel. Grasping the bark with all four paws, he ran swiftly up the tree and clung to a thin branch at the very top. Back and forth he swung in the icy gale, looking like a tiny leaf. Then, as we watched in wonder, he suddenly shot out, spread his feet and sailed down through the tree tops in the high wind. I just hoped he would blow in the right direction.

That evening the wind finally dropped and it was not so cold. Just after 8:30, I looked out the cabin window. Snow was falling softly and in the big feeder I could see one, and then two, flying squirrels! They were sitting side by side, very close together. As they shelled the peanuts and husked the sunflower seeds, I couldn't help wondering if he was telling her about the nights he spent in our cabin.

Snow Stories

On some winter mornings, I could hardly wait to get outside and see who had passed by in the night. The new fallen snow was just like writing paper on which everyone left an autograph. Sometimes there would be complete stories for us to read. Once I found a long line of rabbit tracks that ended suddenly with the imprint of huge feathered wings. A great horned owl had swooped down in the darkness and seized an unsuspecting snowshoe rabbit. I felt sorry for the rabbit, but owls have a tough time in winter when the snow is deep and food is not easy to find.

All through the winter there were lines of tiny footprints around the barn where the mice had ventured out. The tracks showed how the mice never stayed up on the snowy surface for long but scooted down into the network of tunnels they had made beneath the snow where they were safe from hunting owls. It was warmer there too, for snow is like insulation.

One morning when I was up by the barn, I found the imprint of smaller wings in the snow where a heavy body had landed and then a long line of three-toed tracks leading in under a juniper bush. Who could have left such strange marks? I solved the mystery when I lifted the thick branches and found a small depression in the snow where a ruffed grouse had dug itself in for the night, making a snug, snowy cocoon.

Under the old apple tree, the snow was always beaten flat by a cotton-tail rabbit who came to nibble the bark off the lower branches. And sometimes we saw neat little prints running through the hedgerow beside the East Field where an ermine had hunted. I wondered if the tracks belonged to Herman.

I was glad that Rufus, the groundhog, was asleep in his underground burrow because I could see that two coyotes were hunting regularly over the farm. They came out from the wood each night and followed the same route up the lane and across the fields. One time, they left a clear trail of big paw prints right under our bedroom window! I tried howling several times during the winter, but the coyotes never answered. Maybe they were too busy hunting. Or maybe it was too cold.

One frosty morning I snowshoed down to the woods before breakfast and found a line of very mysterious tracks in the middle of the frozen pond. The footprints were small and dainty, and they ran one behind the other in almost a straight line. I knew they had been left by a fox because when a fox is hunting and moving stealthily, it always places its back paws in exactly the same spot as its front paws. The trail looked as if it had been made by a one-legged animal. Following the tracks across the pond, I discovered a scattering of brown feathers. The fox must have flushed a grouse from its roosting place under the bushes at the edge of the pond and caught the bird as it leapt into the air.

The animals' snow stories became harder to read by the end of February. The warm sun was melting the top layer of snow each day and at night it turned into a hard, icy crust. If no new snow fell, it became almost impossible to tell who had passed by while we were asleep. But this was a good sign that the season was changing. Spring was coming and we had new experiences to look forward to.

FOX

WEASEL

SNOWSHOE RABBIT

MICE

COYOTE

Tails after Dark

I glanced up just as the top of a tall, bushy tail passed by under the cabin window. It seemed to wave at me through the glass. Who on earth was that? I ran to the window and peered into the darkness. The outside light was illuminating part of the hedgerow, and I could see something dark climbing up the snowbank. As it moved farther into the light, I saw two broad white stripes running down the centre of its back. The warmer weather had brought out the skunk. I felt sure this had to be the very same one that was living in the old barn along with Porky and the racoon. Only this morning I had found one or two tracks outside the barn door that looked suspiciously like those of a skunk.

We had not seen the skunk since autumn, when we were fixing up the old barn. We knew it was living under the floor, and one night, while John was stumbling about in the darkness, he almost tripped over it. Luckily for John, the skunk was more surprised than frightened and retreated quickly without using his "perfume"! All during the coldest months of winter, the skunk was tucked away in a dry, cozy place somewhere under the floor, not really hibernating, but in a very deep sleep. Now it was the last day of February, the night air was mild, and the skunk was wide awake, very hungry and right under our cabin window.

Climbing up onto the top of the snow bank beside the cabin, the skunk ran back and forth under the suet we had hung from a low branch for the birds. Reaching up, he swiped at it again and again with his front paws, but the juicy suet was too high. Soon he gave up, discouraged, and shuffled off down past the cabin toward the wood. What would he find to eat, I wondered? It was too early in the year for flying insects and last year's grass still lay buried beneath the snow. He could find ant eggs under the tree bark or he could try to catch mice, like the owls. Finding supper was going to take the hungry skunk a long time. We decided to help.

In the cabin refrigerator was a big chunk of stewing beef we had been saving for supper the next day—our supper! I carried the thick lump of meat outside and left it on the snowbank close to the window. The hungry skunk must have smelled the beef clear down to the wood, for no sooner was I back inside the cabin than he reappeared. Around and around he went in circles on the snow until his nose found the fresh meat. Then, holding our supper firmly between his long front claws, he ate hungrily, tearing off great mouthfuls with his sharp little teeth.

The lump of beef grew smaller and smaller as the skunk steadily ate his way through, scarcely pausing to look up and completely unaware that we were watching from the window. Even when I shone the flashlight beam full on him, he didn't stop eating. Nothing was going to interrupt his supper. Except.... who was this coming? As the skunk gobbled down the last few mouthfuls, something small and dark darted out from the shadows at the

corner of the cabin. For a split second I thought it was a
very foolish mouse, but then I realized, in amazement,
that I was seeing the black tip of Herman the ermine's
long tail. His sharp nose must have told him there was
fresh meat around, but surely, I hoped, he was not going
to challenge the skunk for it. I couldn't even guess who
the winner would be in such a contest.

Herman sniffed his way right to the bottom of the
snowbank, then suddenly saw the skunk. For a second he
paused, as if making a quick decision. Then he turned
and ran back, quick as a flash. All I could see was a
black spot disappearing under the window. Herman's
white winter coat was almost invisible against the snow.
The skunk gave no sign of having seen anything at all. He
was busy licking his fingers. I was glad Herman had not
confronted the skunk. I didn't like to think how long it
would have taken to clear the air!

After nosing about on the snowbank to make sure he
had left no meaty scraps behind, the skunk ambled off
down to the woods again, satisfied at last. Now that he'd
eaten our supper, he could take life easy for a while. And
for us, it would be sandwiches instead of stew tomorrow.

Caught in the Act

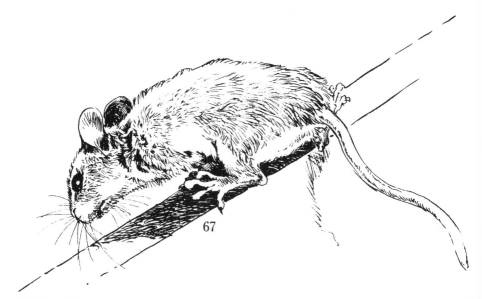

One night in early March something woke me up from a deep, sound sleep. What was it? I lay very still in the darkness, listening, and then it came again; a strange scratching sound, like giant fingernails scraping against wood. In the silence, the noise sounded impossibly loud and I began to imagine a huge, scary creature trying to claw its way into the cabin. I shivered under the blankets and struggled to come fully awake. Was it inside already?

I listened hard and decided that the scratching sounds were coming from low down on the far wall, by the window, and they seemed to be travelling slowly upward. I stared across the room. A small, dark head rose above the windowsill. I sat bolt upright. Something outside was climbing up the cabin wall! I rolled over, felt for the flashlight on the floor and shone it on the window. Two eyes glowed in the beam of light. A masked face was looking in through the glass. I just had time to notice round, furry ears and a pointed black-button nose before the face quickly disappeared. There was a loud slithering noise, a muffled thump, then silence. "What's up?" John called out sleepily. "Nothing's up," I whispered. "It's down. A racoon has just fallen off the window ledge!"

We had not seen the racoon all winter. Sometimes during mild spells we found his footprints in the snow where he had come from the barn to forage for food. I wondered if he ever encountered Porky or the skunk on his nightly forays. The racoon would have slept through the coldest winter months curled up in his warm nest somewhere in the loft of the old barn. With the days and nights becoming warmer now, he would be up and about more often. I only hoped the flashlight had not frightened him away from the cabin.

Partly hidden behind the curtain, I stood and waited by the window. Before long there was a soft scratching on the bottom log. The racoon had come back and was beginning to climb the wall again. I could just see the top of his head coming up over the logs. As his little masked face drew level with the bottom windowpane, the racoon peered into the darkened cabin very cautiously, like a guilty bandit afraid of being caught. No bright light shone out to frighten him this time, and he could not see me standing behind the curtain. Reassured, the racoon crawled along the window ledge and out onto the big tray covered with peanuts and sunflower seeds.

Even in the darkness, I could see that the racoon had lost a great deal of weight. This was not the same

70 roly-poly, mischievous Bandit I had come face to face with last autumn in the barn loft. The winter had been long and hard, but with spring coming, he would soon become fat and healthy again. The peanuts would help. They were full of calories and protein.

Moving to get a better view, I accidentally brushed against the curtain and Bandit looked up, startled. His ears twitched and his pointed nose sniffed the air for signs of danger. His furry stomach seemed so shrunken and thin that I was glad when hunger overcame caution and he went back to the birdseed.

Bandit ran his paws back and forth over the tray, feeling the size and shape of each nut and seed with sensitive fingers, recognizing the food by touch alone.

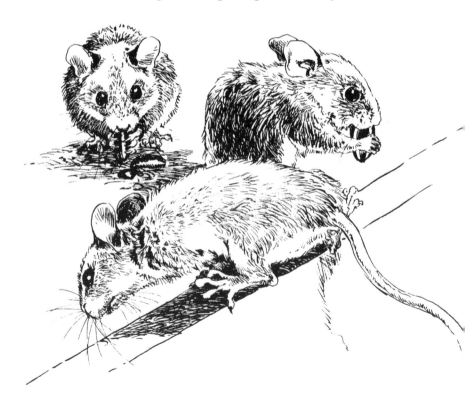

Indeed, most of the time his bright eyes were firmly fixed on the cabin or gazing off into space while his paws did the job of finding supper. I remembered seeing another racoon down by the pond in summer finding his food the same way. He had sat on the bank, staring up into the trees, while his long fingers dabbled expertly about in the water, feeling among the reeds and under the rocks for minnows and crayfish. Racoons don't have to see their food to find it!

By this time Bandit's paws had encountered a shelled walnut among the seeds on the tray. It was easily three times the size of a peanut. What a find! He rolled it over and over between his soft hands, rubbing it as though scarcely believing his good fortune. Then he ate the walnut, sitting up and looking at the cabin window while he chewed. I could see his pink tongue and white teeth. "What a wonderful picture that would make," I whispered to John. But how could we get it? Taking the photograph from inside would be too awkward because the glass panes were so small that the corner of the window would be in the way. We would have to be outside the cabin, and ready, when Bandit arrived. But when would that be? And if the flashlight beam had frightened him, what would he do when the flash on the camera went off?

There seemed to be no easy way of getting Bandit's picture. Then I noticed John looking very thoughtful. "Leave it to me," he said, very mysteriously. "I have an idea."

The next night, we were ready. Outside, John had mounted a camera with flash attachment on the top log just under the roof of the cabin. It was pointed down and carefully focused on the window tray. Best of all, we could operate the camera from inside the cabin by remote control. And the flash was electronic—so the light

72   would flare for less than a split second. With
luck, Bandit would hardly be aware of it. Our
chances of success were suddenly looking
very good. All we had to worry about was
the noise—the sudden "click" as Bandit's
picture was taken and the rapid "zip" as
the electric motor wound the film.

    It was another mild evening and I
was almost certain that
Bandit would come
again in the night.
After supper, we put
more birdseed on the
window tray, and just
to make doubly sure
that Bandit would know
where to come, I hung a
large piece of cheddar
cheese from a long wire
right over the tray. It
dangled down
invitingly. As we went
to bed, I saw the
mice were already
on the tray,
scampering back
and forth like little
grey ghosts.
Whiskers did

not seem too interested in the cheese. He glanced up at
it once or twice, but he was busy collecting all the big
walnuts that we had mixed in with the birdseed for
Bandit.

It was three o'clock in the morning when the racoon
woke us up as he climbed the cabin wall. He must have
smelled the cheese, for as soon as he was on the tray he
looked up at it, dangling above him. John held the
camera switch attached to the long camera cable in one
hand. His finger rested lightly on the button, ready to fire.
I held my breath. Would it work?

Bandit stood high on his hind feet, reached up with
one paw and took a swipe at the cheese.

"Flash!"   "Click!"   "Zip!"

All I saw was the end of Bandit's ringed tail as he
tumbled off the tray onto the snow, scattering birdseed
left and right as he went. The noise of the camera motor
was so loud I heard it clearly from inside the cabin. Poor
Bandit!

A full minute passed. Then there was a faint scratching
sound on the bottom log again. "He must really want that
cheese," I whispered as Bandit's head rose above the
window ledge. This time as he crept onto the tray he
stopped and looked up at the camera very suspiciously.
He knew where the strange noises were coming from. But
when the camera did not move, he soon turned his
attention back to the cheese.

Next time the camera fired, Bandit did not fall
off the tray, at least not all the way off. He was still
hanging on with his front paws and I could see the tips
of his furry ears. Then his masked face appeared and he
pulled himself all the way up. Once more the racoon
gazed up at the camera with inquisitive eyes. It seemed

74   to me that he was less frightened this time, and I hoped he was getting used to the funny sounds.

"Hold your fire," I whispered to John as Bandit stood up and swayed back and forth under the cheese, examining it from all angles. Then he batted it back and forth, first with one paw, then with the other, like a boxer in training. But the cheese was held firmly on the wire and wouldn't fall down. Finally, Bandit reached up as high as he could, fastened all of his fingers around the cheese and pulled hard. "Now!" As the camera fired, the cheese broke apart and fell into Bandit's paws.

I was delighted. We had captured just the picture I wanted. And Bandit seemed pretty pleased too as he sat on the tray, gazing up at the window, and happily munching away on his cheese.

Rufus, Wake Up!

On the first warm day of spring, Rufus woke up from his long winter sleep. The West Field was still covered in snow, but the March sun was quickly melting the last traces away. Big grassy patches were beginning to appear and I could hear the faint tinkling sounds the ice made as it melted into tiny rivulets that streamed down the field. Already huge puddles were starting to form. During the winter, a mound of snow had drifted over the entrance to Rufus' underground burrow and now he had to dig his way out, pushing up through the icy crystals that tickled his nose. That was the moment I saw him, just as he popped out of the snow pile into the early spring sunshine, his eyes blinking in the bright light.

We had not seen Rufus since autumn. He was a much fatter groundhog then, for he had spent the last weeks of summer gorging himself on the alfalfa and rich red clover that grew in the field, eating enough to last him all through the winter. At the end of September, when the fall days grew short and the nights turned cool, Rufus disappeared below ground and curled up in his burrow with his head tucked between his feet. His heart began to beat slower and slower and his body became colder and colder as he slid into the deep sleep of hibernation. I had thought of him often as we skiied and snowshoed over the field, imagining him sound asleep in his winter burrow beneath us. I knew we would not see him until the snows melted, for of all the animals we had encountered on the farm, the groundhogs were the only true hibernators, scarcely stirring until spring.

Now spring had come and Rufus was finally awake. Sitting up on his hind feet with his paws draped over his stomach, he gazed over the field. It looked very different

from the last time he had seen it. The grasses that had
grown so thick and tall around his burrow last summer
lay flat and withered on the bare ground. They didn't
seem very appetizing, and Rufus looked around for
something better to eat. Reaching up, he nibbled a few
bare branches of a bush growing near his entrance, but I
could tell from the way he absently fingered the twigs
that they were not his favourite food. But they would
have to do until the earth warmed up and the fresh
clover that he loved began to grow again.

78   Quickly losing interest in the twigs, Rufus loped around the field, searching for all the other groundhog burrows and digging out their entrances. Perhaps he was looking for a mate. Using his strong front paws, he attacked the wet, heavy snow vigorously, pushing it under him and kicking it into a pile with his back feet. Before long he was wet from nose to tail, and as he bounded over the snowy field, he left a little trail of muddy footprints behind him. But he soon tired, and, climbing up onto a big rock not far from where I was crouching, he stretched out and did what he enjoyed most—sunning himself. The wind ruffled his fur, his eyes closed sleepily, and as the sun moved across the afternoon sky, he turned from time to time, always keeping his back bathed in its warmth.

I moved closer. But the snow crunched loudly and Rufus opened one eye. He could see me quite clearly, kneeling on the wet snow with my camera. But having just come out of hibernation, he seemed slow to react, or maybe he

was too warm and too comfortable to move away. His eye
lazily closed and soon he was asleep again.

Suddenly there was a movement at the far side of the
field. Something–or someone–was slipping silently between
the trees. I caught a glimpse of a small, pointed face,
tufted ears and a rusty red coat that gleamed in the
sunlight. A fox! Lightly, it jumped up onto the cedar rail
fence and scanned the field with sharp eyes. It was
looking right at Rufus! And Rufus was asleep!

Running noiselessly on soft, padded feet along the top
rail, the fox circled the field. When it reached the far
corner, it jumped down and began to move out toward
the unsuspecting Rufus. Closer and closer the fox came.

Already I could smell its strong, musky scent. So busy was the fox stalking Rufus that it did not even see me still kneeling motionless at the side of the field.

Rufus slept on, unaware of the approaching danger creeping steadily and silently toward him. Closer and closer...just a few steps more.... Ears back, the fox crouched low, ready to spring.

"Rufus! Watch Out!"

My call rang out over the field, shattering the stillness. Then everything happened at once. The startled fox leapt into the air, whirled about and raced back down the field, its feet scarcely touching the ground. With one bound, it cleared the fence and vanished into the wood, a blur of rusty red. At the same time, Rufus's eyes flew open, he tumbled off the rock and galloped as fast as his little legs would carry him back to his burrow. Without so much as a backward glance, he dived down the tunnel. Just a few seconds after my warning, the West Field was deserted.

The fox must have been disappointed. It was probably very hungry, having just come through the long winter, and, were it not for me, it might have had an easy meal. I felt a little guilty, for a fox has to eat too, but I just couldn't let him take Rufus. As for Rufus, he would never know how close he came to being supper!

As I walked back to the cabin, I turned and saw the top of a brown, furry head above the burrow and two bright black eyes peering out cautiously. Rufus was wide awake and very alert. I had an idea he would never again be caught quite so sleepy or quite so careless as he'd been on this first warm day of spring.

Fox Watch

Once spring came to Whip-poor-will Farm, we began to have many good sightings of a red fox. Frequently, the fox would pass by the old barn on top of the hill, and sometimes I would see it crossing the wide Centre Field early in the morning. It always seemed the fox knew exactly where it was going, as though it had an important job to do and no time to linger.

The fox travelled across our fields so regularly that we began to suspect it was a female and that she might have a den somewhere in the area, maybe right on our farm. Foxes have traditional trails all across their territory, regular routes they follow all the time. It was clear to us that Whip-poor-will Farm was part of this fox's territory. By using a little detective work, we just might be able to find her den, and the little foxes.

All through the month of April, we kept up a "fox watch," carefully noting when and where we saw the fox each time and marking the exact location on the farm map. Even more important, we drew little arrows to show the direction she was travelling when we saw her. Most of our sightings were either early in the morning or late in the afternoon, and we guessed that the fox was either setting out on, or coming back from, a night's hunting. But we could never predict where she would suddenly appear, and quite often she surprised us. John came face to face with her behind the barn one morning, but she wheeled away so quickly that he did not have time to see if she was carrying food. That would have told us if she was feeding young ones back at the den.

By the end of the month, our map was dotted with a confusing series of x's and arrows. But once we drew connecting lines between them we had a pretty good idea where the fox's main trails were. The three she used

most often all led up into the northwest corner of the
farm. That's where we concentrated our search for the den.

And search we did. Hiking across the small fields, we checked out every rockpile, looked into all the fencerows, peered under brushpiles and combed the deep woods. Every secret hiding place we could imagine was closely examined. I even investigated hollow trees that had fallen down. But we had no luck. Wherever the den was, it had to be very well hidden.

Finally, there was but one place left to search: the big pasture up by the west boundary. It was a long, narrow field sloping down to the woods at one end and bordered on all sides by cedar rail fences. Once the field was good grassland for cattle, but now, judging by the number of

84   burrows, it was mainly a home for groundhogs. It seemed
     an unlikely place for a fox den, and I decided not to
     waste much time checking it out. However, the high,
     grassy hill in the middle of the field would give me a
     good view of the surrounding countryside. We had just
     about exhausted all the possibilities of finding the fox
     den on our farm but maybe I could see locations to
     search on our neighbour's property. I started across the
     bumpy field.

     Halfway to the hill, I sniffed a sudden, very familiar
     foxy scent. It was so strong that I turned, half expecting
     to see the fox lurking in the trees behind me. The musky
     smell was even stronger as I started climbing the hill,
     and then I saw the groundhog burrow in the side of the

hill, a burrow that was far too large for a groundhog!
Around the entrance, the mound of sandy soil was well
worn down by the patter of many feet and there were a
few bare bones lying about, the remains of last night's
supper. I had found the den! The fox had taken over the
abandoned groundhog burrow on the sunny slope, greatly
enlarging the two entrances to suit her own needs. No

doubt, the young kits were in the underground tunnel.

Backing away, I beckoned to John and we hid
ourselves among the bushes behind the rail fence. We
were fairly well concealed and the wind was carrying our
scent safely down the hill away from the burrow. With
luck, the fox would not detect our hiding place. It was
almost three o'clock, so we thought mother was probably

down inside the den with her young kits. If she followed her usual pattern of behaviour, she should emerge around four and set off for the night's hunt. We settled down to wait.

By six o'clock, there was still no sign of any movement around the burrow. It was getting cold and our muscles were cramped from sitting so still on the rocks in the fencerow. We agreed to call it a day. Maybe mother was waiting until dark before she came out. Climbing over the fence, we started down the hill past the burrow. As we walked by, a little furry head popped up suddenly out of the hole...then another...and another...until seven fox pups sat around the den entrance looking at us very curiously. And there we were, caught right out in the open, trying very hard to pretend we were trees!

The fox kits were about eight or nine weeks old we guessed. Their light, sandy coloured coats were already tinged with the dusky red of their mother and they had black-stockinged legs and black tipped ears. They were all fat and healthy looking. Soon, they lost interest in us and began to tumble about, batting one another playfully on the head. Totally absorbed in watching their antics, I jumped when John whispered into my ear, "Don't look now, but here comes mother!"

Sure enough, the adult fox was trotting up the centre of the field straight toward us. Before we had time to decide what to do, she caught our scent, wheeled around sharply and bounded back into the wood. Even at that distance, some silent signal must have passed between her and the young ones, for when I looked back at the burrow, there was not a pup in sight. Mother fox had certainly fooled us and upset all our careful calculations! But we would try again.

Next day we took up our positions behind the fence
much later in the afternoon so that we would not have
so long to wait. Foxes keep such regular habits that I
fully expected she would return to the den at the same
time again. Determined to see her the moment she
stepped out from the trees, I scanned the wood continually
through binoculars, while John kept watch for the young
ones at the burrow.

Fooled again! At six o'clock mother came up out of
the burrow, stretching and yawning widely in the sunlight.
She had been down inside the whole time! The pups all
popped up again and played as before, hiding behind
rocks and pouncing on one another in mock ambush,
learning through play the hunting techniques they would
need later when they were on their own. They pulled
mother's ears and bit her tail, trying to persuade her to
join in their fun, but the fox seemed distracted—and very
suspicious. Frequently she lifted her head to sniff the
wind and looked over toward our hiding place in the
fence. She knew something was not quite right. We dared
not whisper to each other or even change our positions,
no matter how uncomfortable, for fear of making a noise.
Her hearing was too good!

As the pups played about the hill, the fox kept careful
watch over them. In the weeks ahead, she would begin to
lead them away from the den each day, showing them
how to catch mice and teaching them how to fend for
themselves in the wild. By the end of summer, the pups
would head out on their own. If they survived the cold
winter, they would be raising families of their own
next spring.

Now the fox was standing up, no longer looking in
our direction but down the field toward the wood. The
breeze ruffled her gleaming russet coat and she looked

very lean, with no spare fat anywhere on her slim body. Still staring intently toward the wood, she began to pace back and forth nervously, as though she was expecting someone. Who? Even the pups seemed to catch her changed mood, stopping their play and gazing off into the distance. As the shadows began to lengthen across the fields, the fox became more restless still, and then, through the binoculars, I saw who she was waiting for. A second fox had emerged from the trees and was moving up through the field. The dog fox, father, was bringing home supper. Dangling from the corner of his mouth I could see the long, thin tail of a muskrat.

The male fox came up the field at a fast trot. I waited expectantly to see what would happen when he arrived at the burrow. Would all seven pups fling themselves on the dead muskrat or would they wait patiently to be fed one by one?

Near the bottom of the hill, the dog fox stopped

abruptly and stared over at our fence. Perhaps he could see our outline against the setting sun as we crouched low behind the rails, or maybe he had caught our unfamiliar scent. In any case, he whirled around and ran lightly all the way back down the field to the wood. I didn't have to look at the burrow this time to know there would not be a mother or fox kit in sight. The father's actions were a clear warning signal. The family responded instantly. We moved quickly away, not wanting to keep the hungry pups waiting.

Back at the cabin, we looked again at our farm map with all its carefully drawn x's, arrows, and lines. No wonder our calculations had been wrong. We had been assuming all along that there was only one fox when there had been two, both hunting at different times! "Never mind," I said to John. "We'll probably need a new map next spring anyway. Who knows, maybe there will be seven more fox dens to find!"

Mrs Rufus

May is my favourite month on the farm. The fat buds on the maple trees are all popping into leaf, the clover is up in the fields and the days are warm and sunny. The swallows are back; so are the orioles and rose-breasted grosbeaks. Every morning we are awakened by a dawn chorus that the robins begin as early as four o'clock and every night we listen to the calls of the whip-poor-will.

Violets and trilliums bloom in the woods, chipmunks rustle the dead leaves in the hedgerows, and down at the pond below the cabin, hundreds of frogs sing out in springtime chorus. Brightly coloured wood ducks cruise along the shoreline, and two very secretive mallards look for good nesting places at the far end of the pond, well away from our prying eyes. A pair of muskrats is busy building a house of reeds and grasses at the side of the pond, and down at the Secret Lake the beaver are out and looking for poplar branches once again.

In springtime, it seems that everything is waking, growing, returning, blooming, building, eating or singing! There is a new life, new colour and new sounds – like the sound of Porky chewing our cabin logs! We had wondered how long it would take him to discover them. One night he started working his way through the bottom log by the back door. In the darkness and the stillness, his teeth sounded like giant chisels cutting through the wall. We had to discourage him. He wanted to sample the oak door sill as well, but after we chased him off he gave up and turned his attention to the fresh green clover in the East Field. He had lots of company out there. One morning I counted five porcupines.

The skunk was around every night now, and once or twice I saw Herman the ermine slipping between the logs

in the outside woodshed. I did not recognize him at first,
for he had turned completely brown. Without his white
winter coat he was not nearly so distinguished looking.
The snowshoe rabbits looked different too. Their summer
fur was growing in and only a few white patches were left
on their hind legs and long ears. Against the dark forest
floor, they showed up like patches of leftover snow.

It was good to know that our friends who shared
Whip-poor-will Farm had survived the cold winter. But
there was still someone we had not seen in a while, at
least not since that warm day in early March. Where was
Rufus? The clover he loved was growing all around his
burrow, but there was no sign that his home was in use.
Had the fox frightened the groundhog away? Or, even
worse, had the fox slipped
back and caught him
later?

Our worries were soon
over. While John was putting
up bluebird nesting boxes in the
Centre Field one afternoon, he spied
Rufus sitting up on a big limestone boulder
in the hedgerow sunning himself. There was a freshly
dug burrow under the old apple tree in the middle of the
field. Rufus had moved his home.

Next day, after taking off the storm windows and
putting on the screens, I followed Rabbit Trail through the
wood to the Centre Field, hoping to catch sight of Rufus
in his new neighbourhood. I didn't see Rufus, but I did
see a coyote! At first I thought a grey dog was stalking at
the edge of the field, but there was no mistaking those
long legs, pointed nose and bushy tail. All thoughts of
Rufus vanished, and in my excitement all I could think
about was making contact once again with a coyote.
Could I make it respond to me as the whole family had
done last autumn?

Dropping to my knees, I crouched low until not even the top of my head was showing and began to howl. The coyote looked up, surprised. I howled again, and then again, but he would not respond. Maybe it was the wrong time of day for howling. But the coyote was clearly very interested in knowing what was making such a strangely familiar sound. Unable to see me through the tall grass, he began to jump up and down as though he were on a spring. With each jump, his head rose higher and higher. I sank even lower, hoping the coyote would become so curious that he would come right over. I had no such luck. This coyote was more cautious than curious. A few moments later, he disappeared through the fence rail.

Now I began to think about Rufus again. Had the coyote been hunting him? There was no sign of the groundhog at the new burrow and I began to worry. Surely I had not saved Rufus from a fox in March only to have him eaten by a coyote in May! But no. There was Rufus, half buried in clover at the opposite side of the

field. He looked fat and healthy and from the way he frequently stood up and peered around, Rufus was in no danger of being caught unawares again.

Reassured, I stretched out on the warm rocks under the apple tree and lay back to enjoy the sun as much as Rufus did. My eyes closed—and then I suddenly had the strangest feeling that I was being watched. Cautiously, I half-opened one eye. I *was* being watched—by not one but four miniature Rufuses, each one an exact copy of father! They were among the rocks where I lay, and when I slowly sat up one came and placed his tiny paw against my knee, as though wondering what this big, unfamiliar object was. Then they all began to play right beside me.

Moving even more slowly, I reached for my camera. What a wonderful chance to take pictures! But it wasn't easy. The babies were too close and they would not hold still long enough to have their pictures taken. Finally, squinting through the viewfinder, I had one beautifully in focus and was all set to press the shutter when something big moved in the background. Peering over the top of the camera, I found myself confronting a very suspicious looking Mrs. Rufus!

Well, there was no point in pretending to be a tree—at this range Mrs. Rufus would know the difference. So I just tried to stop breathing. For what seemed an eternity, but was probably just a second or two, we gazed at each other. Now, I thought, she will turn and dive down the burrow, taking all the babies with her. But Mrs. Rufus didn't. Right at that moment one of the youngsters came barrelling over the rocks, rushed at mother, and began bunting her in the stomach with his head. He wanted a drink! Momentarily distracted, Mrs. Rufus gave her baby a few rough licks with her tongue and then let him suckle. With his paws pressed against her fur and his eyes tightly shut, the baby groundhog contentedly drank away, making little gurgling noises that I could hear quite clearly. Mrs. Rufus appeared to have completely forgotten about me, or maybe she had simply accepted my presence. Whatever the reason, it was my good fortune.

Once his thirst was satisfied, the young groundhog scampered back to play with the others, and Mrs. Rufus, ignoring me, sat up and nibbled the grasses around the rocks. From time to time she stopped eating and carefully cleaned herself, licking her paws all over and using her claws like combs to groom her fur. Finally, she turned her back and moved a short distance away. Climbing up onto the top of a granite boulder overlooking the field, Mrs. Rufus settled down comfortably in the sun and began to keep a coyote watch. And I spent the next hour baby-sitting!

Stranger in the Nest

"Fee be, fee bee, fee be." There was no mistaking the clear calls coming from the top of the lilac tree. The pair of phoebes was back and trying to find a way into the barn. Quickly I ripped away the last of the clear plastic that had covered the barn windows all winter, and the little female bird zipped right in and perched on top of the big beam. Her long tail wagged up and down as she carefully inspected the familiar surroundings, looking for a good nesting site. Perhaps she would add on to last year's nest, or take over one of the empty swallow nests, or maybe she would build a new one on an upstairs rafter.

The phoebes had flown halfway up the continent to reach our barn, all the way from the southern United States, where they had spent the winter. They made the long journey every year and the farmer who sold us our land told us phoebes had been nesting in the barn for as long as he could remember, and that was close to forty years. What a good thing we had not torn the barn down!

One morning, not long after we had seen the two phoebes at the barn, I flung open the kitchen curtains and saw yet another phoebe hovering in front of the window. I had an idea what she was looking for. All around the cabin she flew, checking out every hidden beam, nook and cranny, and peering in at me through every window. She was searching for a secluded place to build her nest. I could hear her mate calling "fee be, fee be" from the hedgerow as he announced to the whole world that our cabin was now their territory!

The two birds must have been raised in the old barn last spring when our cabin was nothing more than a pile of logs lying in the field. Now they were back, fully grown and ready to raise a family of their own. And what a

surprise for them to discover there was a new building
on the farm. One thing was certain: if the phoebes liked
our log cabin well enough, they would come back to nest
year after year.

The cabin had all kinds of places to build nests, some
good and some not so good. Our Phoebe was determined
to inspect them all. First, she chose to build on the beam
right above the front door, but we had to discourage her
from there. Our continual comings and goings would be
sure to cause a disturbance. Next she selected the beam
right over the back door, and we had to discourage her
again for the same reason. But tucked up under the edge
of the roof above the small north window was an ideal
spot, well hidden. To make it even more suitable for her,

John nailed up a little ledge to help support the nest. Then we waited anxiously, wondering if she would approve of the place we had picked out for her.

On her next circuit around the cabin, Phoebe flew up under the edge of the roof and perched on a long rafter right above the new ledge. From inside, looking through the window, I watched as she carefully inspected our handiwork, cocking her head from side to side and flicking her long tail up and down. It was hard to tell what she had decided when she swooped away, but when she returned, she was trailing a long strand of fine grass!

Phoebe began to weave her nest right in the middle of the small ledge that John had nailed up for her. Back and forth she flew, bringing in grasses and mud from the pond in her beak. As she worked away, her mate sat calling high in the trees, defending their territory. Phoebe never liked us watching her build, and if she saw us peeking out through the window, she would fly down and hover right in front of the glass as if to say, "I know you are there spying on me." We had to stop using the back door altogether.

Once the nest was completed, Phoebe began to lay her clutch of small, white eggs, one egg a day until there were five. After the last egg was laid, she began to brood, keeping them warm all night and during most of the day. Now it was just a matter of waiting.

Two weeks later, all five eggs had hatched and we could see the downy little heads rising above the side of the nest. Both parents became very busy now feeding the new family. Phoebes are flycatchers and there were more than enough insects to satisfy the hungriest of the nestlings. They grew very quickly. Soon there was no room for mother in the nest at night and she had to perch on a nearby beam.

By June, the young phoebes were large enough to leave the nest. They all fledged on the same day, heading for the hedgerow and soon flitting expertly from branch to branch as though they had been flying all of their lives. As we stood quietly under the trees, we could hear their high-pitched cheeping calls like little radio beacons telling the parent birds where they were. Phoebe and her mate continued to bring food to them, stuffing wriggling caterpillars and large moths down their open beaks. We could always tell by the excited chirpings when a feeding was taking place. But the fledglings would not be dependent for long. In a week or two they would be catching insects on their own.

With her five young ones successfully hatched, raised and launched, I thought Phoebe deserved a holiday. But she had other ideas. The same day that her babies fledged, Phoebe was back rearranging the nest. She was getting ready to lay more eggs! Little did she know that her second family was going to be very different from her first!

In the days that followed, I did not want to worry Phoebe by constantly checking her nest, but a sign of trouble appeared when I found two broken egg shells on the ground. Who had been the thief? The red squirrel that sometimes raced over the cabin roof? Another bird? Or could it have been Whiskers or Tuffy? I knew that mice would steal small eggs, but it seemed unlikely that they could have found Phoebe's hiding place under the edge of the roof. We could only hope that she would lay more eggs and not abandon her nest.

Every morning, after first making sure that Phoebe was not around, I slipped out the back door of the cabin and checked to see if there were any new eggs. Standing on tiptoe and holding a small mirror above the nest, I could see in easily without causing any disturbance. But the nest remained empty. Both phoebes were still flying about with the members of their first family, who by now were almost as big as they were. In fact, when they all lined up side by side on the garden fence, it was difficult to tell them apart. Perhaps Phoebe had decided one family was enough after all.

When I had almost given up all hope that Phoebe would lay more eggs, they suddenly started to appear again in the nest. By the end of the week there were five, and Phoebe was brooding them exactly as she had done before. All seemed well, and we waited expectantly for the second family to appear.

Another three weeks went by. Surely the eggs should have hatched by now, I thought, but we could see only one small downy head in the nest. Where were the other four? For some reason, only one egg had hatched. I felt sorry for Phoebe, but at least she had one chick and it would be very well looked after.

In the days that followed, the baby chick began to grow—and grow. It grew to be as big as Phoebe, and then even bigger! And then we knew what had happened to Phoebe's second family, for sitting in the nest and becoming larger every day was not a phoebe chick but a baby cowbird! There had been large groups of cowbirds in the hedgerow all spring. One of them must have discovered Phoebe's nest under the roof, whipped in the moment she was off the nest, destroyed her eggs and laid in their place a single − larger − cowbird egg. Our two phoebes had become foster parents!

We soon learned that baby cowbirds are not nearly

so independent as baby phoebes. Long after this one had finally fledged from the nest it continued to sit in the hedgerow like a large helpless lump waiting to be fed. And when it came to flying, the cowbird was a very slow learner! Nevertheless, Phoebe and her mate did not abandon the chick, even when it became almost twice their size, but continued to look after it as carefully and as conscientiously as if it had been their own. And, in a way, it was. The five chicks from Phoebe's first nesting still flew around the cabin and, come fall, they would make the long journey south together. Next spring, the birds would all be back – two phoebes, five grownup phoebe chicks, and one cowbird. A fine family!

108

Looking Back

Almost before we knew it, summer had come and we were celebrating the end of our first year at Whip-poor-will Farm. The oats stood tall and golden in the fields once more and wild grape vines spread in tangled confusion along the fence rails. The farm looked much the same as it did when we first pitched our tent and began to look for a cabin site, but now I knew every trail, every little field and every leafy glade. The farm had become very familiar—and so had all its wild inhabitants.

For most of the birds, the spring nesting period was over and the male birds no longer sang quite so loudly and vigorously to defend their territories. The farm seemed quieter and more still. The foliage grew so thick and lush in the woods that it was much harder to see the small wild creatures that live so close to us. But they are still there. Every time I walk through the forest, I

can almost feel the hidden eyes watching me pass by.

Now, at the height of summer, there is less activity around the cabin. Porky has decided to move out of the barn and return to the wood. A good thing too, for it will give us a chance to repair the foundation wall in his corner of the basement—and to sweep out all the porcupine quills!

The skunk and the racoon have also departed. The skunk has taken up summer residence under the stonepile in Juniper Field, but Bandit has not gone nearly so far. On warm, humid afternoons I can usually find him curled up sound asleep in the arm of the old maple tree beyond the gate, his hind feet tucked under him and his little masked face resting comfortably across folded paws.

And every time I follow Rabbit Trail, just at dusk, I peer up into all the big trees, hoping to see the familiar faces of our two flying squirrels peeking out from some deep cavity. They stopped their nightly visits to the cabin in April after we took down the winter bird feeders. But they will come back in the autumn.

Even life in the cabin is quieter. In the spring, Whiskers turned out to be a Mrs. Whiskers. She raised her large family in the bottom drawer of an old chest under the stairs, using one of John's thick winter sweaters to make a nest. We did not discover it until much later, after the babies had grown up and were scampering about on the shelves. But what with Tuffy, Misca, and all the others, there were too many mice living in our basement. We caught and released them all into the fields and hedgerows where they really belonged. Of course, most of them came right back. Even now, as I write, I can hear the faint sound of someone chewing in the basement. I have no doubt it's Whiskers. But we don't mind. After all, what would a log cabin be without deermice?

At the end of our first year we can look back and remember all the wildlife adventures we have had, and they are certainly not over! Only yesterday, as I was picking daisies below the cabin, I turned and found myself staring into the hazel-brown eyes of a young coyote, almost full grown. And John has discovered the tracks of a big black bear up on High Ridge Trail.

After our year on Whip-poor-will Farm, I will never again think of a farm as just a place for horses, cows and sheep. It is much more than that. Now, every time I drive past a field I look for groundhog burrows. And when I see an old barn, I always wonder if there is a racoon asleep in the loft or a porcupine living in the basement. Farms are homes for all kinds of wild creatures.